THE REAGAN ERA

AMERICAN ERAS: DEFINING MOMENTS

T0021585

MARTIN GITLIN

CHERRY LAKE PRESS

Published in the United States of America by Cherry Lake Publishing Group
Ann Arbor, Michigan
www.cherrylakepublishing.com

Content Adviser: Kevin Whinnery, MA, History
Reading Adviser: Beth Walker Gambro, MS, Ed., Reading Consultant, Yorkville, IL
Photo Credits: © Courtesy Ronald Reagan Library, cover, 1; © Wikimedia/Released by the Reagan
    Library, US National Archives, 5; © Gerd Eichmann/Wikimedia, 7; © Rawpixel Ltd/Photo by Carol M.
    Highsmith's America/Flickr, 8; © National Archives Catalog/NA Identifier 12008442, 9; © National
    Archives Catalog/NA Identifier 6728684, 10; © Adrienne Wallace/Dreamstime, 13; © Wikimedia/John
    C. Hylan Houses in Bushwick, Brooklyn, 14; © National Archives Catalog/NA Identifier 75852891, 15;
    © Lane V. Erickson/Shutterstock, 16; © The U.S. National Archives/Picryl, 17; © Photo by PH3 David
    Travis/Picryl, 19; © Cliff/Flickr, 20; © Photo by US Navy/Wikimedia, 21; © National Archives Catalog/
    NA Identifier 75854473, 22; © Everett Collection/Shutterstock, 25; © National Archives Catalog/
    NA Identifier 75855873, 26; © NEW HOPE/Shutterstock, 28

Cherry Lake Press is an imprint of Cherry Lake Publishing Group.

Library of Congress Cataloging-in-Publication Data
Names: Gitlin, Marty, author.
Title: The Reagan Era / by Martin Gitlin.
Description: Ann Arbor, Michigan : Cherry Lake Publishing Group, [2022] | Series: American eras:
    defining moments | Includes index.
Identifiers: LCCN 2021007807 (print) | LCCN 2021007808 (ebook) | ISBN 9781534187429 (hardcover) |
    ISBN 9781534188822 (paperback) | ISBN 9781534190221 (pdf) | ISBN 9781534191624 (ebook)
Subjects: LCSH: United States—Politics and government—1981-1989—Juvenile literature. |
    Reagan, Ronald—Juvenile literature.
Classification: LCC E876 .G565 2022 (print) | LCC E876 (ebook) | DDC 973.927092—dc23
LC record available at https://lccn.loc.gov/2021007807
LC ebook record available at https://lccn.loc.gov/2021007808

Cherry Lake Publishing Group would like to acknowledge the work of the Partnership for 21st Century
Learning, a Network of Battelle for Kids. Please visit http://www.battelleforkids.org/networks/p21
for more information.

Printed in the United States of America
Corporate Graphics

ABOUT THE AUTHOR

Martin Gitlin has written more than 150 educational books. He also won more than 45 awards
during his 11-year career as a newspaper journalist. Gitlin lives in Cleveland, Ohio.

TABLE OF CONTENTS

INTRODUCTION

Most Americans were ready for a change when the 1980s arrived. Many believed the country was headed in the wrong direction.

They had plenty of evidence. Mistrust of the government remained high. It had only been 5 years since a **scandal** forced President Richard Nixon to be the only president ever to resign. Gas prices had soared in the 1970s. The economy was struggling. And 52 U.S. hostages continued to be held captive in Iran. Iranian revolutionaries took the hostages because they felt that the United States had too much influence over their government.

Americans wanted desperately to feel more confident about their nation. Some thought President Jimmy Carter wasn't up to the job. They believed he was overwhelmed by the many problems the country faced.

A former actor named Ronald Reagan gave them hope. He ran against Carter in the 1980 presidential election after serving as governor of California. The **conservative** Republican talked about the return of optimism. He appealed to a sense of **patriotism** in the American people.

Ronald Reagan was the 40th president of the United States.

The resulting election was a landslide. Reagan beat Carter handily. The hostages were released the same day he took office. Many credited his tough talk against Iran for their freedom.

Reagan wasted little time putting his policies into effect. Americans argued whether they helped or hurt the nation. What is certainly true is Reagan helped launch a conservative movement that Republicans embraced for decades.

CHAPTER 1

Reaganomics

One of Reagan's primary goals was to bring back a strong economy. He faced many problems when he took office. Many people were out of work. The **inflation** rate had nearly doubled over the previous 2 years. Americans were looking for fresh ideas.

Reagan had a plan. He set out to cut **taxes** to give people more money to spend. He also sought to **deregulate** industries. One result was that **corporations** no longer needed to spend large sums of money to avoid polluting the air or water. Clean air standards for car manufacturers were lowered.

The idea behind that strategy was that big businesses would save money. They would then use that savings to create jobs, gain profits, and boost the economy. It would also lower prices for consumers.

The economy was not doing so well in 1980,
as inflation rates were very high.

Almost 17 million new jobs were created under Reagan.

Unfortunately, the income gap between the rich and everyone else in the United States continued to increase.

Reagan's economic policies had mixed results. The unemployment rate dropped drastically. One in eight, or 12.5 percent, of Americans were out of work in 1980. In 1982, unemployment dropped to 11 percent. And by 1983, only 8 percent of Americans were out of work. Unemployment continued to remain low throughout Reagan's 8 years in office.

Reagan made efforts to reduce Medicaid grants, a state-run healthcare program for the impoverished, resulting in many losing out on benefits.

But many people continued to struggle. While unemployment rates fell, poverty increased. Reagan boasted that he was anti-government. He believed that Americans were better off with little government control. This meant many government programs that provided resources to low-income groups were cut like Social Security, Medicaid, and food stamps. The wealthy and middle classes thrived, while those who needed government programs suffered.

The Moral Majority

Many **evangelical** Christians believed the United States was heading in a poor moral direction. Baptist minister Jerry Falwell formed the Moral Majority in 1979. He wanted this organization to influence and steer American politics back to "traditional values." The Moral Majority supported Ronald Reagan and helped elect him to the White House. However, Reagan was a former Hollywood star. His first marriage had ended in divorce. When he was governor of California, he passed a bill that was for **abortion** instead of against it. These issues weren't in agreement with the Moral Majority's values. But that didn't matter because they supported Reagan's many other policies, including his stance on **communism** and limited government. Would you support someone who you didn't completely agree with? Why or why not? Give an example and discuss your thoughts with a family member or friend.

CHAPTER 2

The Homeless

Americans saw a disturbing sight before and after Reagan became president. They saw people living on the streets. Many were upset because they felt Reagan didn't address this issue appropriately during his time in office.

It was estimated that between 200,000 and 500,000 people were homeless during the Reagan administration. One reason was his cuts on **social services** that were put in place after the Great Depression during which there were an estimated 2 million people who were homeless. Many of those living on the streets suffered from mental illness and **substance abuse**. These people weren't able to receive help for their conditions. And without that help and support, they stood almost no chance of holding a steady job to pay for housing.

There were Vietnam veterans, children, and laid-off workers who were homeless as a result of Reagan's budget cuts.

In Reagan's first year in office, he cut the budget for public housing in half to about $17.5 billion.

Other factors created by Reagan policies contributed to the unfortunate increase in people becoming homeless. One was the high cost of housing. Some people simply couldn't afford home **mortgages** or rent.

Many Americans felt Reagan didn't care about the poor. The president believed in what is known as "trickle-down economics."

Reagan gave many interviews where it appeared
he was indifferent to those who were homeless.

Some of the social programs Reagan cut were Social Security, Medicaid, food stamps, and education programs.

Reagan increased military spending by 43 percent.

The theory is that helping the wealthy creates opportunities for others. His trickle-down policy seemed to work as the 1980s recession ended. But many others were negatively affected. The strategy left poor people behind.

Another blow to the economy was an exploding **deficit**. Reagan had promised to cut government spending, and he did. He cut domestic programs, like social services. But he increased spending for the military. The result was that the national **debt** nearly tripled.

CHAPTER 3

Big Bucks for Bombs

President Reagan launched the biggest military defense buildup in U.S. history. He served in the Army for 8 years and believed that a strong military equaled a strong country. He increased military spending by $30 billion in 1981. It then increased every year he was in office. The defense budget rose from $138 billion to $304 billion from 1980 to 1989.

Some of the added funds were used to build high-tech weapons systems, increase military pay, and offer more training opportunities. Reagan believed a powerful military was a **deterrent** to war. He felt it prevented other countries from posing a threat against the United States.

Reagan wanted to build up the military to protect
the country from communism.

Part of Reagan's buildup included the Strategic Defense Initiative, also known as the Star Wars Defensive Missile program. This was to protect the United States from a nuclear attack.

Some Americans disagreed with that idea. They had grown tired of military spending during the Vietnam War, which he ended less than a decade earlier. They felt that building up the military threatened world peace. They also pointed out that spending billions on the military increased the **federal** deficit.

As a result of the increased spending, new weapons such as B1 bombers and stealth technology were being developed.

Reagan and Soviet leader Mikhail Gorbachev met in 1985 to discuss cutting back on nuclear weapons.

Others welcomed an increased defense budget. They believed their country had become weak. They later said that Reagan's military policy helped destroy communism in Eastern Europe and end the Cold War with the **Soviet Union**.

The relationship with the Soviet Union indeed improved under Reagan. But it can be argued that this change had nothing to do with the increase in the military budget.

The Day After

About 100 million Americans planted themselves in front of their television sets on November 20, 1983. They tuned into ABC for a movie titled *The Day After*. It has remained the most watched TV movie in American history. It depicted a nuclear attack on the United States. The film followed the lives of fictional people in Kansas who were trying to survive after the bombs fell. Do you feel it was a good idea for ABC to air such a scary and realistic drama? Why or why not? Share your thoughts with a family member or friend. What do they think?

CHAPTER 4

Thaw in the Cold War

It was June 12, 1987. President Reagan was giving a speech in West Germany. Nearby was the Berlin Wall. It was built in 1961 to stop people in Communist East Germany from escaping to **democratic** West Germany.

Reagan targeted his words to Soviet leader Mikhail Gorbachev. The two had developed a friendly relationship. Hope had replaced fear. People around the globe yearned for an end to the Cold War. They dreaded the nuclear arms race between the two nations that threatened the entire world.

The Berlin Wall was a concrete barrier that divided
Berlin from 1961 to 1989.

The president knew that the Berlin Wall **symbolized** the
Cold War. So he asked Gorbachev to break down the barrier
between the Communist and democratic worlds. "Mr. Gorbachev,
tear down this wall!" he said to the cheers of the crowd.

Whether those words played a role in the wall coming down
2 years later is up for debate. The people of East Germany and
other Eastern European countries had tired of Soviet control
and the restrictive Communist system. They forced change.
Soon, communism was gone in those countries.

The Intermediate-Range Nuclear Forces (INF) Treaty of December 1987 did not cover sea-launched missiles.

Gorbachev also worked to give his people greater freedom. He met many times with Reagan to improve relations with the United States. The goal was to reduce the nuclear **arsenals** of both countries. That goal was realized in December 1987 when the two leaders signed a treaty to limit the number of missiles they had stockpiled.

The Cold War was over. Americans felt more at ease about the future of the world. And many believed they had Ronald Reagan to thank for it. Today, however, the United States still has tensions with Russia for some of the same reasons that kept the Cold War burning for years after World War II.

The Wall Comes Down

Ronald Reagan was no longer president when the German people joyfully tore down the Berlin Wall. George H. W. Bush was in office on that fateful day of November 9, 1989. It came 5 days after 500,000 East Germans gathered in East Berlin for a mass protest against their Communist government. Their leaders tried to appease the people by loosening travel restrictions to West Germany. But the spirit of freedom had overtaken East Germans. Germany reunited as one country less than a year later. How do you think the German people felt when the Berlin Wall came down?

Many believe that Reagan did not appropriately address homelessness during his 2-year term.

Research & Act

A 2017 estimate revealed that there were more than 500,000 homeless people in the United States. Research where and how homeless people are living in your community. Then, find out ways that you can help them, including donating food and serving them meals. Learn about the organizations that work to house and feed the homeless. Then, discuss it with your parents or teachers. Talk about organizing a campaign with your friends or classmates to help the homeless.

[21ST CENTURY SKILLS LIBRARY]

Timeline

November 4, 1980: **Ronald Reagan defeats Jimmy Carter and wins the presidential election.**

January 20, 1981: **Reagan is inaugurated as president, and the 52 American hostages held in Iran are released.**

February 18, 1981: **President Reagan gives a speech about increasing defense spending and decreasing spending on social programs.**

March 30, 1981: **President Reagan is shot in the chest outside a hotel but survives.**

August 13, 1981: **The Economic Recovery Tax Act is signed into law.**

October 2, 1981: **President Reagan announces plans for military buildup.**

January 6, 1983: **The gasoline tax increase is signed into law.**

November 6, 1984: **President Reagan is reelected in a landslide defeat against Walter Mondale.**

November 19 and 20, 1985: **Soviet President Mikhail Gorbachev meets with President Reagan in Geneva, Switzerland.**

December 8, 1987: **President Reagan and Gorbachev sign a historic treaty limiting nuclear weapons.**

Further Research

BOOKS

Benge, Janet, and Geoff Benge. *Ronald Reagan: Destiny at His Side.* Lynwood, WA: Emerald Books, 2010.

Joshua, George. *The Cold War Explained: Pocket History for Kids.* Independently published, 2019.

Medina, Nico. *What Was the Berlin Wall?* New York, NY: Penguin Workshop, 2019.

WEBSITE

Ducksters—Biography: President Ronald Reagan
https://www.ducksters.com/biography/uspresidents/ronaldreagan.php

Glossary

abortion (uh-BOR-shuhn) medical termination of a pregnancy

arsenals (AR-suh-nuhlz) collections of weapons

communism (KAHM-yuh-nih-zuhm) a system of government with single-party control of production

conservative (kuhn-SUHR-vuh-tiv) political belief that supports established institutions and customs

debt (DET) money owed to someone else

deficit (DEH-fuh-suht) having more expenses than income

democratic (deh-muh-KRAH-tik) relating to democracy, a system in which the supreme power is held by the people

deregulate (deh-reh-gyuh-LAY-shuhn) removing rules or restrictions

deterrent (dih-TUHR-uhnt) something used to prevent a bad outcome

evangelical (ee-van-JEH-luh-kuhl) closely following the teachings of the Bible

federal (FEH-duh-ruhl) related to the national government

inflation (in-FLAY-shuhn) a rise in prices over a long period of time

mortgages (MOR-guh-jez) agreements for monthly payments in buying a home

patriotism (PAY-tree-uh-tih-zuhm) strong feelings for the country in which one lives

scandal (SKAN-duhl) dishonest or immoral action that disgraces those associated with it

social services (SOH-shuhl SUR-viss-uhz) government programs that help people

Soviet Union (SOH-vee-uht YOON-yuhn) a federation made up of Russia and several other smaller countries

substance abuse (SUHB-stuntz UH-byoos) a medical disorder in which people use a drug excessively

symbolized (SIM-buh-lized) stood for or represented something else

taxes (TAK-sez) money collected by the government to fund its services and programs

INDEX